NEW CRAFTS

DECOUPAGE

NEW CRAFTS

DECOUPAGE

25 handcrafted projects shown in 280 step by step photographs

MAGGIE PRYCE

Photography by Nicki Dowey

LORENZ BOOKS

To Adrian and Niki for their unstinting support and encouragement.
With special thanks to Katy for being a wonderful assistant during
the writing of this book.

This edition is published by Lorenz Books,
an imprint of Anness Publishing Ltd,
108 Great Russell Street
London WC1B 3NA

info@anness.com

www.lorenzbooks.com;
www.annesspublishing.com

If you like the images in this book and would
like to investigate using them for publishing,
promotions or advertising, please visit our website
www.practicalpictures.com for more information.

© Anness Publishing Ltd 2013

Publisher: Joanna Lorenz
Project Editor: Simona Hill
Photographer: Nicki Dowey
Step Photographer: Rodney Forte
Designers: Lilian Lindblom and Lucy Doncaster
Illustrators: Lucinda Ganderton and Madeleine David

ACKNOWLEDGEMENTS
The author and publishers would like to thank the following artists
for the projects and gallery pieces photographed in this book:
Belinda Ballantine: p13; Penny Boylan: p36, p74;
Sandy Bryant: p42, p46, p63, p66, p86, p91;
Chest of Drawers/Lucinda Ganderton: p28, p44,
p50, p58, p69, p72; Alison Jenkins: p38, p82;
and Tamara von Schenk: p15.

Thanks to Chris Mann for the blank wooden candlestick; Buckleys
Ironwork for the shell doorknobs on the Nautilus Bathroom
Cabinet; and Gallery Five, London for the Victorian toys wrapping
paper (design by Claire Windteringham 1995) and the fruit and
flowers wrapping paper (design by Nicola Rabbett 1995).

PICTURE CREDITS
The publishers would like to thank the following for permission to
reproduce pictures in this book:
British Museum: p8, p9 left and right; the Mary Evans Picture
Library: p10 left and right, p11; PhotoArt: p14 top left, top right and
bottom right, p15 top left.

CONTENTS

INTRODUCTION

The French word 'decoupage' originates from the verb 'decouper' meaning 'to cut', and describes the craft of using paper cut-outs to decorate anything from a tiny box to a large piece of furniture.

In its most basic form, decoupage involves cutting out a chosen image, sticking it on to an object and then varnishing it with as many coats as possible to give depth and to create the illusion that the design has been painted on. The beauty of decoupage is that anyone can try it and, even using the simplest of designs, can create something to be treasured. No specialist skills are required except an eye for colour, balance and design, which we all draw on when decorating our homes and choosing our clothes.

For many people the best aspect of decoupage is the opportunity it provides to produce an original artefact from paper, prints and glue, that looks as if it has been painted. One of the greatest compliments that a decoupage design can invite is the exclamation: "I thought it was painted on!"

Opposite: Wrapping paper, copyright-free designs and cuttings from magazines are all good sources of decoupage material.

HISTORY OF DECOUPAGE

Decoupage became enormously popular in Europe in the late 17th and 18th centuries, following the development of trading links with the East. It was out of favour at the beginning of the 19th century, but in Britain in the Victorian era it became an extremely fashionable pastime once again for well-to-do ladies. Current interest in decorative period furniture has promoted the craft.

With the opening up of trading routes to China in the 17th century, the Dutch East India Company began importing lacquer-ware and porcelain to Europe alongside spices. In 1682, Louis XIV was presented with a red lacquer-ware table by the ambassador from Siam. Nothing like it had been seen before, and it was not long before it became all the rage. Such was the demand among the nobility for pieces of painted lacquer-ware, that European furniture-makers started to imitate Asian lacquer-ware, or 'chinoiserie' as it became known.

Famous artists had their original designs sketched on to panels and screens to be tinted by apprentices. However, demand became so great that designs were soon mass-produced. Apprentices cut, tinted and glued sketches to panels, screens, tables, boxes and other items of furniture, which were then lacquered. In Venice, this technique became known as 'lacca contrafatta'.

Such was the passion for this new art that court ladies all over Europe took up decoupage as the latest hobby, cutting up anything they could lay their hands on, as this early 18th-century letter written by a Mme Aisse illustrates: 'We are here in the height of a new passion for cutting up coloured engravings....Every lady, great and small, is cutting away. These cuttings are pasted on sheets of pasteboard and then varnished. We make wall panels, screens, and fireboards of them. There are books and engravings that cost up to 100 lire apiece. If this

fashion continues, they will cut up Raphaels!' Indeed, in France, Marie Antoinette and her court ladies were doing just that as they snipped away at originals by famous artists such as Boucher and Fragonard. A piece of decoupage done by Marie Antoinette in 1780 is inscribed with the words: 'Découpure faite par la Reine', which translates as 'Decoupage by the Queen'.

In England the technique of painting lacquer-ware was known as japanning. In 1762 Robert Sayer published a book of over 1,500 decoupage designs 'for joining in groups or to be placed singly'. These had to be 'neatly cut round with sicsars (sic) or the sharp point of a knife...brushed on the back with strong gum water or thin paste'. Next, seven coats of 'seedlac' (varnish) used, although 'twelve are better still'.

Above: This illustration depicts an 18th-century print room. Typical of the period, the walls are lined with rows of black and white prints.

Above: On first viewing, this stylized piece looks like a watercolour artwork, but look closer at the design and you will see that each leaf, petal and twig has been carefully cut from hundreds of tiny pieces of coloured paper and then pasted into place. Mary Delany, the creator of this work and over 1,000 others, was a prominent figure in fashionable Victorian society. Her work was highly acclaimed for its botanical accuracy and attention to detail. On occasions she incorporated pressed leaves into her designs, although they are hard to distinguish from the paper replicas she so carefully crafted.

Left: Like decoupage, the fashion for things Chinese has waxed and waned over the centuries. This lacquer chest features inlay work requiring a high degree of craftsmanship.

In 1772 Mary Delany invented a new hobby for herself, 'flower collages'. Like most well-to-do ladies of her time, she had always occupied herself with a range of leisure pursuits and was highly accomplished at embroidery, shellwork and landscape painting. She was a keen gardener and numbered among her friends some well-known botanists. Working from real flowers, she cut tiny pieces of coloured paper in the shape of the petals, leaves and all other parts of the plant. Her skill was to use different shades of the same colour, as would an artist. She would then stick them (with, it is believed, egg-white or flour and water) on to a black background. The pieces were layered to build up a picture, taking hundreds of pieces to make up one plant. Mary Delany was 72 years old when she

Right: Folding screens lend themselves to decoupage and were popular subjects for decoration in both the 18th and 19th centuries.

Below: Sentimental images appealed to Victorian taste. Flowers were favourite motifs for decoupage and, when used on small gifts or 'tokens of affection', sometimes had symbolic meanings.

began this new hobby, and over a period of ten years she made over one thousand paper 'mosaiks', as she called them. These exquisite flower collages are now housed in the British Museum in London.

Print rooms were another way to display 18th-century decoupage. They were often found in grand British country houses, where an entire room would be decorated with original prints, sometimes brought back from fashionable tours to France and Italy. Prints of similar sizes were positioned in symmetrical rows covering almost the entire wall surface. They all had cut-out border frames and

were glued directly on to the walls, with paper ribbons, swags and bows joining them together. Prints in such rooms usually had a common theme running through them.

By the early 19th century the passion for Asian lacquer-ware had declined. It was to reappear in the Victorian era in another guise when 'scrap' screens decorated with cut-outs of fairytale characters, children and animals became popular. These large folding screens were found in Victorian children's nurseries, and the cut-outs were usually applied randomly to completely cover the surface.

During the Victorian period, mass-produced sheets of brightly coloured, embossed paper scraps were printed to provide people with ready-made motifs. These took the form of popular Victorian favourites such as valentines, cherubim, costume fashions and flowers. Victorian ladies kept albums in which they stuck paper cut-outs alongside pieces of verse. These were far from being simple scrap books, however. Writing in 1938 in her book *Silhouettes*, Mrs E. Nevill Jackson described these sophisticated books as: 'Delightful old albums where perfumed valentines, hearts and darts, coloured scraps and miniature landscapes were gummed down by our great-aunts and grand-mothers…many a treasure may be found hidden between the leaves of the scrap album.'

Towards the end of the 19th century, decoupage briefly flourished again in the form of 'potichomanie' (from the French *potiche*, meaning 'vase' and *manie*, meaning 'craze'). The idea was to imitate Dresden and Chinese porcelain by gluing printed paper scraps on to the inside of a glass vase. The vase was then painted inside to give it a background colour. After this period decoupage again went into decline, then has reappeared at intervals as interest in it revived.

The re-emergence of this craft is perhaps due to two factors. Firstly, an alternative to the stripped pine look may have precipitated a move towards decorative effects on walls and furniture. Secondly, easy-to-use, quick-drying water-based products has made decoupage easier. The choice available to the decoupage artist has grown hugely, with companies selling blanks (items such as wastebaskets, trays and boxes that are bare and ready to decorate). This allows you to choose a specific object to decorate, rather than having to search for a junk store find.

Decoupage today takes many forms. The original black and white designs used in the 18th century and Victorian scraps are now available in copyright-free books. As a result there are styles to cater for all tastes. But beware – for those who take it up, decoupage can very easily become a passion just as it did amongst the court ladies in 18th-century France and Italy!

Right: The colourful image of Santa Claus and his bag of presents was a popular subject on ready-made Victorian scraps.

GALLERY

The art of a successful decoupage design is in tricking the eye to believe a design has been painted on to the surface of an object, rather than cut out and pasted into place. The designs illustrated below demonstrate that decoupage can be worked in many styles on almost any prepared surface, large or small, and with a huge range of source material.

Above: IVY LEAF VASE
A terracotta garden pot disguised with cream paint is behind this elegant large vase. A classical design of black and white swags, bows and tassels is complemented with colourful images of orchids. The whole design has been aged with crackle varnish.
Sandy Bryant

Right: FLORAL BEDSIDE TABLE
This bedside table was a simple, bland MDF (medium-density fiberboard) blank before it was covered in this brightly coloured wrapping paper.
Chest of Drawers

Left: NOAH'S ARK
CHEST
*Marine life provides a
wealth of inspiration
for all craft subjects,
and has been used to
colourful effect on this
storage chest.*
Chest of Drawers

Left: HAT BOX
*Floral images are
always a popular
decoupage choice.
This idea shows how
easily portraits can
be incorporated into
decorative decoupage.*
Josephine Whitfield

Above: GILDED
BOWL
*Images by Nicholas
Hilliard were applied
to the surface of this
glass bowl. Imitation
Dutch metal leaf was
applied over the
remaining surface
area which was
then distressed to
appear aged.*
Belinda Ballantine

Right: JEWELLERY
BOX
*Working on a small
scale with tiny images
will test the skill of
any decoupage artist.
A classical border
lends a touch of
grandeur to this
whimsical box.
Guild of Decoupers*

Above: HAND
MIRROR
*Motifs are cut out
from ornate wrapping
paper and used to
decorate a plain
mirror.*

Top: CLOCK
*A simple clock is
decoupaged with cut-
out Victorian images,
which are glued onto
a plywood base, then
varnished.*

Left: TOILET SEAT
*An ordinary pine toilet seat forms the basis of
this cheeky design. Copyright-free images of
cherubim have been antiqued, then pasted to a
painted background. The surface has been aged
with crackle varnish and several layers of
varnish applied to provide a hygienic finish.
Maggie Pryce*

Above:
DECORATED MATS
New mats are treated
with a paint effect
and decoupage
decoration. The
background creates
an impression of raw
silk, to complement
the Chinese print.
Elaine Green

Right: SEAT
A technicolour chair
has been created
using an array of
colourful papers. The
papers are torn into
even pieces, wrapped
around the chair then
glued into place.
Sandra Hadfield

Above: DANCING
BEES BOX
The bees encircling
this painted box have
been cut out of folded
paper like a row of
dancing dolls.
Emma Whitfield

Below: CLOCK
A surreal decoupaged
clock of an angelic
face with fish floating
by. The powerful
image is enhanced by
the use of just black
and white.
Josephine Whitfield

MATERIALS

The most important materials in decoupage are printed images to cut out. These can be from magazines, wrapping paper or copyright-free books. Various kinds of paints and varnishes are used for the background, for ageing and tinting, and to seal the finished work.

Abrasive paper comes in various grades from fine to coarse. Use it to remove blemishes before painting, and to 'key' a surface to help paint to adhere. For decoupage the finer grades are less likely to damage the design.

Acrylic paints are used to tint black and white prints. They come in a wide variety of colours, and can be used neat or diluted with water or an acrylic medium.

Black and white prints can be used as they are or can be tinted with coloured pencils or artist's paints.

Copyright-free books are a good source of decoupage material.

Dutch metal leaf is imitation gold leaf. It is less expensive than real gold leaf and is easier to apply. It is essential to seal it to prevent tarnishing; the colour is improved by sealing with shellac. It is available loose (between leaves of tissue paper) or attached to waxed paper.

Emulsion glazes are used over a painted background to produce a translucent, broken colour, effect. Mix equal amounts of paint and PVA or water-based varnish, then add two to four parts of water.

Emulsion (latex) paints are used to paint backgrounds. They are water-based and come in a huge range of colours, in both matt (flat) and silk finishes.

Gilt wax comes in shades of gold and silver and is useful for highlighting intricate mouldings and edgings.

Glue stick is used to attach cut-outs, especially when gluing paper to paper.

Kitchen paper is useful for clearing spillages, protecting surfaces or as an aid to distress gold leaf.

Magazines are full of images. Test a piece first to ensure that the print does not show through from the other side.

Methylated spirits (alcohol) are used for cleaning brushes that have applied spirit-based products. They are also used to dilute shellac and sanding sealer.

Oil-based varnish is slower-drying than acrylic varnish. It is harder and more heat-resistant than acrylics, but does yellow over time. It is used where an antiqued effect is required, or as a final protective coat.

Oil paints are used for highlighting the cracks in a craquelure finish and for antiquing. They are slow-drying.

Paint stripper is caustic and must never come into contact with the skin or eyes.

Primer is used to seal bare or new wood. It also helps the new coat of paint to bond with the surface. Acrylic undercoat is fast-drying and will take oil- or water-based paint on top. Old metal surfaces require red oxide primer, which inhibits rust.

PVA (white) glue is white but dries clear. It is fast-drying and should be diluted with water to make it spreadable (one part PVA to two parts water). As it is water-soluble, cut-outs can be soaked off from the background even when they are dry.

Reusable adhesive can be stuck to the back of cut-outs when planning designs.

Shellac is a toffee-coloured, spirit-based lacquer used to seal bare wood, to age paintwork, and to tint and seal prints. It will seal a layer of Dutch metal leaf and prevent tarnishing.

Tack-rag is made of gauze impregnated with oil. It is used to remove dust particles. Store it in a sealed plastic bag.

Two-step crackle varnish produces a finish which imitates the hairline cracks found on old oil paintings. It is available in a pack of two bottles, designed to be used together.

Victorian scraps are still available, either in books or in sheet form.

Wallpaper paste is slower drying than other glues, allowing more time for cut-outs to be repositioned.

Water-based acrylic varnish is very easy to use and, where many layers of varnish are required, is ideal because it is quick-drying. Another advantage is that it is not necessary to sand between layers of varnish, unless there are visible trapped dust particles. The only disadvantage is that brushmarks can sometimes remain visible, so use as fine a brush as possible.

Water-based size is a fast-drying adhesive used in gilding. It has a milky appearance, which turns clear when the size has reached the correct tackiness – about 20–30 minutes after application.

Wax gives a patina to a finished piece.

White spirit is used to clean oil-based products off brushes. It is added to artist's oil paint to dilute it and can also be used to distress Dutch metal leaf.

Wire (steel) wool must be the finest grade available. Use it to remove old wax and to distress Dutch metal leaf.

Wood filler, sometimes called plastic wood, is used to fill any holes and cracks in wood where a smooth finish is required. The best are those that require a separate hardener to be mixed in.

Wrapping paper is available in good department stores.

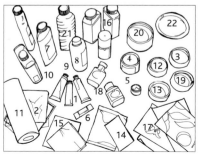

Key

1 Oil paint
2 Dutch metal leaf
3 Emulsion glaze
4 Metal primer
5 Gilt wax
6 Glue stick
7 Methylated spirits (alcohol)
8 Water-based size
9 Acrylic paint
10 Paint stripper
11 Kitchen paper
12 Paint

13 PVA (white) glue
14 Reusable adhesive
15 Abrasive paper
16 Shellac and sanding sealer
17 Source material
18 Two-step crackle varnish
19 Water-based acrylic varnish
20 Wax
21 White spirit (paint thinner)

22 Emulsion (latex) paint

EQUIPMENT

The craft of decoupage requires very little equipment to get started – in fact, most of it is general household equipment that can be found around the home, or purchased at reasonable cost. Small, sharp-pointed scissors are essential to cut out the motifs and borders accurately and a gilder's mop (tip) will be useful if you intend to use Dutch metal leaf.

Artist's paintbrushes A medium or small paintbrush is used to apply glue or paste to the back of cut-out motifs. A medium paintbrush is used to tint black and white prints and photocopies.

Coloured pencils are used to tint black and white prints and photocopies. Watercolour pencils are also suitable.

Craft (utility) knife Used to mitre corners and for other accurate cutting. Always use with a cutting mat.

Cutting mat Essential when using a craft knife to protect the work surface.

Decorator's paintbrushes Various brushes are needed for painting, varnishing and applying size. Choose an appropriate brush for the object and keep separate ones for each task. Clean immediately after use – water-based paints such as emulsion (latex) can be cleaned in water, oil-based paints should be removed with a proprietary brush-cleaner.

Decorator's brushes are used for painting and varnishing. The larger the object you are working on, the larger the brush you require, but for most projects a 2.5cm (1in) brush is suitable.

Gilder's mop (tip) This extremely soft brush is used to smooth down gold leaf after it has been applied and to remove the surplus leaf. A very soft brush can be used instead.

Masking tape is very useful for temporary positioning, and also to mask off areas such as mirror glass to prevent paint and glue splashing on to them.

Metal ruler Used with a craft knife to cut straight lines and to mitre corners.

Scissors A small, sharp-pointed pair of scissors is needed to cut out motifs and borders. A larger pair is useful for cutting away excess paper.

Sponge A natural sponge is used to wipe off excess glue or paste after sticking down a design. It is also used to apply a glaze. A sponged background is achieved by dabbing on layers of different-coloured paint to create a mottled effect.

Tweezers (not shown) are very helpful for picking up delicate cut-outs that may be damaged if you pick them up with your fingers.

Wire brush This very stiff brush is required in order to remove rust from old metal objects to prepare the surface for decoration.

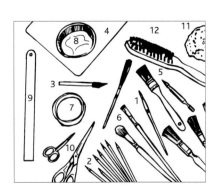

Key
1 Artist's paintbrushes
2 Coloured pencils
3 Craft (utility) knife
4 Cutting mat
5 Decorator's paintbrushes
6 Gilder's mop (tip)
7 Masking tape
8 Metal foil containers
9 Metal ruler
10 Scissors
11 Sponge
12 Wire brush

BASIC TECHNIQUES

The range of items you can decorate is endless. Ready-made blanks are readily available, which require only the minimum of preparation. Glass, metal, wood, china – even plastic – are all suitable surfaces that can be decorated with decoupage. Avoid decorating valuable or antique items, or old wooden pieces with a beautiful natural patina.

SURFACE PREPARATION

Preparation is extremely important and should never be overlooked in your impatience to start. It is vital to have an absolutely smooth surface to work on if you are to achieve a 'painted on' look. If a surface is not prepared thoroughly, problems can occur later that could ruin your hard work.

Painted Wood

If painted wood is in good condition, all you need to do is to 'key' the surface using abrasive paper to enable further coats of paint to adhere. Wipe down with warm, soapy water and leave to dry. Apply a layer of undercoat, sanding lightly when dry, followed by two layers of your chosen colour.

If the wood is in poor condition, it is best to remove the paint, using a paint stripper, and to start again.

New, untreated wood and MDF (medium-density fiberboard)

If the wood is to be painted, apply a coat of primer. When dry, lightly sand the surface, then apply two coats of paint. If you want to leave the wood grain visible, seal the surface with shellac first.

Waxed surfaces

Remove any wax, or the paint will not adhere. Dampen a wad of wire (steel) wool with white spirit (paint thinner) and apply to the surface, working with the grain.

New metal

Scrub with warm, soapy water and allow to dry. Apply red oxide primer, which will act as a rust retarder and 'key' the surface for the paint. If your paint is pale, apply one or two layers of acrylic primer.

Rusting metal

Brush off loose rust with a wire brush and, if necessary, abrasive paper. Then scrub thoroughly with soapy water. Apply red oxide primer and two coats of emulsion.

PAINT FINISHES

Decoupage can be enhanced by a decorative background. The following paint finishes are all easy to achieve.

Sponging

This simple technique can be done using just paint, or by mixing paint with a glaze for a more subtle, translucent effect. A darker shade can be sponged over a slightly lighter background, or vice versa. If you choose the latter effect, the easiest way to lighten the background colour for the top coat is to mix it with a little white paint. Two or more colours can be very effective.

Paint on the background colour and let it dry. Dampen a small, natural sponge with water, squeezing out any excess. Dip it into your chosen colour and dab off any excess paint on a piece of kitchen paper. Lightly and randomly dab (not wipe) the sponge over the surface. The sponging can be sparse or intense, depending on the effect you want to achieve.

Sponging – alternative method

To achieve a more translucent effect, mix the second coat of paint with some glaze. To make an emulsion glaze, mix equal parts of emulsion (latex) or artist's acrylic paint with PVA (white) glue or water-based varnish, then add a little water to make the desired consistency. A good solution is one part glaze to four parts water. Allow the paint to dry and finish with a coat of water-based varnish.

Dragging

This is another translucent effect that uses an emulsion glaze. The glaze is dragged on so that the base coat shows through. This effect looks best on smooth wood rather than old, damaged pieces – MDF is ideal for dragging. Mix up an emulsion glaze using equal parts of water-based paint and PVA or water-based varnish, then add about two to four parts water and stir well. This glaze dries fairly quickly so is best used on small items. Drag the glaze on in parallel lines. If you want a more pronounced effect, take a dry paintbrush and drag it over the surface again, taking care to wipe excess glaze off the brush as you go. Leave to dry.

PAINTING EDGES AND RIMS

On objects such as boxes, firescreens, trays and tablemats, a painted edge defines and finishes the piece beautifully. Pick out a colour from the design that will contrast with the base, or perhaps antique gold to lend a sophisticated look. Painting a freehand line is not difficult, provided you use the correct brush - a 'coachliner' (liner). The bristles are all the same length as they are designed to hold the paint rather like a pen. This enables you to paint a reasonable distance without having to constantly replenish the paint. It is advisable to paint any lining before sticking down your design. Practise on a piece of scrap paper until you are happy with your efforts. Have a damp cloth to hand to wipe up any mistakes.

1 On a small plate, mix some artist's acrylic or emulsion paint in your chosen colour with a little water, making enough to form a small pool. To make antique gold, use a small amount of gold and raw umber artist's acrylic paint with a little water, mixing well until no lumps remain. Add tiny amounts of colour at a time, mixing until you achieve the shade required.

2 Dampen your brush slightly and lay it in the pool of paint, turning it over to ensure that all the bristles are covered.

3 Holding your brush like a pen, lay it right up against the edge of your object. Standing away from the object and using the edge of your hand as a support, drag the brush towards you, using your little finger as a balance. Towards the end, gradually lift the brush up so that it doesn't drag over the edge. If you need to reload your brush, gradually lift it up, fill with more paint and continue, overlapping the lines to ensure continuity. Then leave to dry and, if necessary, apply another layer of paint for better coverage.

Above: 'Antique' gold paint adds an opulent touch to any decoupage item.

GILDING

Adding luxury to decoupage, gilding provides a wonderful base on which to display an intricate cut-out, and will lift a more simple one. As the gilding in this book is used for a background effect and is not being applied to an antique object, Dutch metal leaf is used rather than real gold leaf, which is more expensive and more difficult to use.

1 Paint the base with a layer of acrylic primer. Leave to dry, sand lightly, then use a tack-rag to remove any dust particles. Then paint on two coats of reddish-brown emulsion (latex) paint, sanding and tack-ragging after the second coat to ensure a smooth surface.

2 Paint on a thin layer of water-based size, making sure that all areas to be gilded are covered. Leave to dry for 15–30 minutes until the size appears clear.

3 Remove a sheet of leaf from the book – do not remove its waxed backing. Try not to handle it too much; you may find it helps to wear cotton gloves. If necessary, cut the square of leaf with sharp scissors to a size marginally bigger than the area you want to cover. Gently lift the leaf by its backing and lower it on to the surface. Check its position carefully as, once it is laid, it cannot be repositioned. Press the leaf down by smoothing over the backing with your fingers, then lift off the waxed paper and discard. Cover the remaining areas in the same way, cutting the leaf and overlapping the joins.

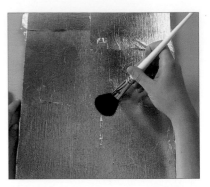

4 Once you have covered the piece, take a gilder's mop (tip) or a wad of cotton wool (cotton balls) and smooth over all surfaces, paying attention to the overlapping edges. These should be smoothed over in one direction only. Attempt to remove the lines where the leaf joins as much as possible. At this stage, the aim is to ensure that all the leaf has adhered, rather than to remove any surplus.

5 Leave the size to dry thoroughly overnight. Then use the gilder's mop to remove the surplus leaf with a light circular brushing motion. If there are any bare areas, these can be covered by first applying size. You can then either lay on more leaf or, alternatively, apply bronze powder with a brush. Bronze powder is particularly useful if you want to colour small folds and intricate mouldings.

DISTRESSING GOLD OR METAL LEAF

You may find that the colour of the leaf is a little bright. If so, you can distress, antique or decoupage the finish – or a combination of all of these. The following techniques are easy ways to achieve a distressed or antiqued look.

1 Take a small wad of fine-grade wire (steel) wool and gently drag it along the leaf in one direction, concentrating on areas where there would naturally be wear and tear. You may not see much difference at this point, but do not be tempted to overdo the distressing.

Take a piece of paper towel, moisten it with white spirit (paint thinner) and gently wipe it over the areas you have distressed, removing the grey particles of wire wool to reveal the undercoat. This can be done as lightly or heavily as you wish. Leave to dry before sealing.

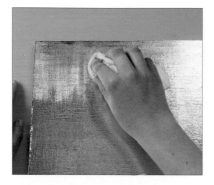

2 For a random look, moisten a wad of kitchen paper with white spirit, as before. Wipe over the parts to be distressed, continuing until the leaf starts to come off. Allow to dry, then seal.

ANTIQUING GOLD OR METAL LEAF

Unlike distressing, antiquing does not involve the removal of leaf. Instead paint is brushed on and removed in parts.

Mix raw umber acrylic paint with a tiny amount of water. Brush it on in one direction, wait a few minutes, then wipe off the surplus with kitchen paper, wiping in one direction. This leaves a slightly streaky appearance. For a more obviously dragged look, a flat brush, slightly dampened, can be used to remove the surplus paint. Allow to dry and then seal.

SEALING DUTCH METAL LEAF

Dutch metal leaf consists of copper and zinc and must therefore be sealed to prevent it from tarnishing. The sealing must be done before starting the decoupage. Spirit-based lacquers are excellent for sealing leaf. Sanding sealer is virtually colourless, whereas shellac tints the leaf and enhances the colour, making it appear more like real gold.

Make sure the shellac or sanding sealer is well mixed. Brush on an even coat, ensuring that all areas are well covered. Try to avoid going over an area twice, or the first layer may start to lift off. Watch for runs and remove them as soon as possible, as both these lacquers dry very quickly. Clean the brush immediately in methylated spirits (alcohol). Allow to dry for about an hour before decorating with the decoupage design.

TINTING AND SEALING PRINTS

Black and white prints and photocopies can be used on their own, but they can also benefit greatly from a tint to lessen the somewhat stark look. They can be antiqued with shellac or tinted very simply using artist's acrylic paints or coloured pencils.

Antiquing prints with shellac

Add a little shellac to some sanding sealer and mix this with a small amount of methylated spirits (alcohol), until you achieve the desired shade. Test it on a piece of paper first. Bear in mind the area that you need to cover and mix an appropriate amount, as it may be difficult to match the tint if you run out. Brush a thin layer of the mixture over the print, laying it on in one direction and overlapping the layers to ensure that you get complete coverage. This method also seals the print. When you have finished, clean your brush with methylated spirits.

Tinting using artist's acrylic paints

Mix a small amount of paint with a little water, then add other colours as necessary. Test the colours on scrap paper. When you are satisfied with the colour, lightly shade in the pale areas, then move on to the darker areas, increasing the intensity of colour.

Tinting using coloured pencils

Start with the lighter shaded areas first, using light strokes in the same direction. Gradually build up the colour, blending it carefully to erase demarcation lines.

Sealing tinted prints

Once tinted prints have dried, brush a layer of sanding sealer over the surface. Clean the brush with methylated spirits (alcohol).

CUTTING OUT

Whether you prefer to use a pair of scissors or a craft (utility) knife, the basic principles remain the same. Always use a cutting mat with a craft knife.

1 Taking a larger pair of scissors, first cut the excess away from around the outer edge of the image.

2 Cut away any areas from the centre of the design. Using the point of a pair of small scissors, pierce a hole in the area you want to cut away, then cut around the edge. Cut away the outer edge of your design. Do not leave any edges of the paper showing – if necessary cut slightly inside the edge of the motif. If you are cutting out an intricate area, leave a small connecting strip as support and snip it away just before you glue.

GLUING CUT-OUTS

PVA (white) glue is the most common method and is suitable for gluing cut-outs to most surfaces. Wallpaper paste is another popular option, especially for larger designs. Mix the paste following the manufacturer's instructions and remove excess paste as described below. For small decoupage designs a glue stick can be used, especially if the background is paper or thin card (stock).

If you are working with PVA glue or wallpaper paste, it is advisable to cover your work surface and to allow yourself plenty of space.

Use a small roller to press out excess wallpaper paste from underneath large sheets of paper or borders, and also to ensure there are no trapped air bubbles.

Using PVA glue

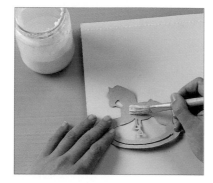

1 Add a little water to some PVA glue to make it spreadable. Using an artist's paintbrush, spread some glue on the wrong side of the cut-out. Thinly cover the entire surface. Alternatively, brush the glue on to the surface of the object, especially when gluing a large, or intricate piece. Always remove any surplus glue.

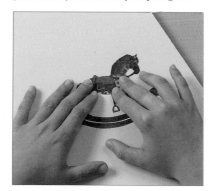

2 Press the cut-out on to the surface, starting at the centre and working outwards. If working on a small item, hold your work up to the light to highlight any imperfections. Lift any edges that have been missed and dab on glue. Leave for a few minutes, then, using a barely moistened natural sponge, wipe away excess glue from around the motif. Leave to dry.

MITRING CORNERS

If your decoupage design has a cut-out border with corners, cut the borders so that they are slightly longer than the edges.

1 Mark the centre point of each edge lightly with a pencil. Centre the border, using the pencil mark as a guide, and stick down the centre portion of the border only, leaving the ends free. Do the same with all the remaining edges.

2 Place a metal ruler at 45 degrees across the angle where two of the borders overlap, ensuring that the ruler lines up with the corner.

3 Using a craft knife, cut through both borders at once. Lift off the surplus paper, then glue down the corners.

CRACKLE VARNISH

A crackle finish imitates the fine, random cracks on old oil paintings. Practise on a piece of scrap wood. Apply plenty of layers of varnish, so that if it does go wrong and you have to remove it, you won't damage the design.

Apply the slow-drying ageing varnish, then, after the specified time, apply the fast-drying water-based crackle varnish. Once the top layer is dry, it cracks as the slow-drying base varnish underneath continues to dry. The trick is learning the right time to apply the second layer. Once the cracks have formed, they should be highlighted so that they stand out. Raw umber is the most common colour used, but you can experiment with other colours – for example a pale colour over a darker background. Terre verte and Payne's grey paint are also effective, and metallic powders can be brushed into the cracks.

1 Brush on a layer of the first stage of the ageing varnish. This must be applied in a medium thickness and evenly, so that no patches are left uncovered. Check that it is completely covered, then leave to dry for anything between 1–3 hours, depending on humidity and temperature. Test it by lightly touching the surface with your fingers; it should feel dry but slightly tacky.

2 Brush on a layer of the second stage, the 'crackle' varnish, working evenly and in one direction. This second layer should be dry in 1–2 hours. When it is completely dry, hold it up to the light to see if any cracks have appeared.

3 If no cracks appear run a hairdryer on its coolest setting over the surface, not too close. Stop as soon as the cracks appear. If you are unhappy with the finished effect, remove it with a cloth soaked in water and start again.

4 Rub some artist's oil paint into the cracks to highlight them. Don't use water-based paint as it will lift the top layer of varnish. Mix a little oil paint with a little white spirit (paint thinner) to make a thin paste. Using a circular motion, wipe this mixture all over the surface using kitchen paper or a soft cloth.

5 Wipe off the surplus paint with a clean piece of kitchen paper, so that the colour is just left in the cracks. Leave overnight to allow the oil paint to dry thoroughly. Finish off the piece with 1–2 layers of oil-based varnish.

ANTIQUING

The most common method of antiquing a piece of decoupage is to use raw umber paint, which gives an aged, dusty look. First apply a couple of layers of water-based varnish over the decoupage.

Mix a small amount of paint with its appropriate solvent – that is, white spirit with oil paint or water with emulsion. Try out the effect on scrap paper first to check the colour. To make it darker or lighter, just add more paint or water. Paint a layer of the solution on to your project. Don't worry about runs at this stage.

Leave it for a few minutes (allow a little longer if using oil paint), then using kitchen paper, wipe off the solution, leaving a residue around the edges of the decoupage and in corners. If you are not happy with the effect, remove it with kitchen paper or with white spirit.

VARNISHING

Varnish will protect your cut-outs, give depth and create the illusion that the design has been painted on. Stir the varnish well with a clean old wooden spoon before using. Dip your brush into the varnish, about halfway up the bristles. Lay the varnish on in light strokes, working in one direction only. Go over a few times, replenishing your brush, until you have completely covered the area. Do not apply too much varnish at a time as this can cause runs.

Check your work a few minutes after you have finished and brush out any drips. If you find a run that has already dried, wait until it is hard, then slice it off with a craft knife. Sand gently and continue varnishing. Clean your brush in the appropriate solvent.

The number of coats required partly depends on the thickness of the cut-outs and whether some are overlapping. In general, the thicker the design, the more coats you will require. Hardwearing items such as trays or children's furniture will need more varnish. As a guide, use a minimum of five coats and a maximum of fifteen coats.

There is a bewildering array of varnishes to choose from. The best choice is to use matt (flat) acrylic varnish to build up the layers, then finish with a few coats of oil-based varnish to protect the piece. Ensure that the room in which you are working is dust-free, and don't wear anything with wool fibres.

TROUBLE-SHOOTING

Air bubbles

Using a very sharp craft knife, carefully cut a slit in the bubble, where possible following the contour of the design. With the point of the knife, gently lift up the edges of the cut and, using a fine brush, fill the slit with some glue and press down.

Tears

Once thin paper has been glued, it becomes very fragile. Tears can also occur when you are sticking very delicate pieces such as flower stems.

If you have a spare matching piece, cut it out and stick it on top of the torn one. Alternatively, remove the torn piece with a craft knife and replace it. You can also glue a different, larger cut-out on top of the tear, for example another flower if it is a floral pattern.

BEADED TIE-BACK

This tie-back looks striking against plain curtains. Several coats of clear nail polish give each bead a glossy lacquered effect that is very decorative. The same technique could also be used to make personalized jewellery.

2 Cut out several small motifs from another sheet of paper. Glue them randomly on to the bead, then seal with a coat of diluted PVA glue.

1 Tear small fragments of paper and glue them to each bead, using an artist's paintbrush. Overlap the edges to cover the bead completely.

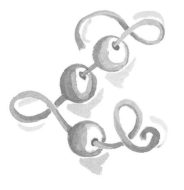

4 Repeat as necessary until you have the required number of beads. Thread the beads on to a length of cord and knot both ends.

3 Give the bead a lacquered finish by painting it with several layers of clear nail polish. Allow each coat to dry completely before applying the next.

Materials and Equipment You Will Need

Patterned origami paper • Large wooden beads • PVA (white) glue • Medium artist's paintbrush • Small scissors • Clear nail polish • 1m (1yd) contrasting cotton cord

ROSE BOX

This little trinket box with its pretty posy of roses provides ideal storage space for small pieces of jewellery, while at the same time adding a feminine touch to a dressing-table. Crackle varnish gives the rose design a lovely antique look.

1 Remove the box lid. Paint a layer of acrylic primer over the box. Leave to dry. Lightly sand the surface, then follow with two coats of cream emulsion paint.

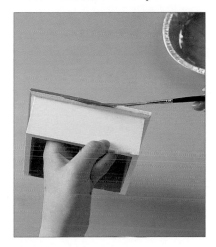

2 Prepare antique gold paint by mixing a little raw umber and artist's gold acrylic paint with a touch of water. Using a coachliner brush, lay the brush in the paint and ensure it is well covered. Place the brush on one edge of the box rim and drag it along to the end. Paint all the edges on the base and lid in the same way. Leave to dry. Follow with an even layer of water-based acrylic varnish to protect the base colour.

3 With small scissors, cut out the rose-heads, making sure that you choose colours that complement each other. Use a different design for the front and sides.

4 Measure the width and length of the box lid with a ruler to find the centre. Mark this point with a pencil. Mix some PVA glue with a little water and brush it on to the back of the first rose. Stick it in the centre of the box lid, then add the rest, one at a time, around the central rose until you have a circle.

5 Fit the lid on to the base but don't screw it back together. Apply the designs to the back, front and sides, sticking your motifs over the join (seam) of the lid and base. Leave the box to dry.

6 Place a metal ruler along the edge of the join over which you have stuck the motif and draw a very sharp craft knife along the join, making sure that you cut cleanly through the paper. Repeat on the other two sides.

Materials and Equipment You Will Need
Small wooden box • Screwdriver • Small decorator's paintbrush • Acrylic undercoat • Fine-grade abrasive paper •
Cream emulsion (latex) paint • Artist's acrylic paints in raw umber and gold • Coachliner (liner) brush • Water-based acrylic varnish •
Rose motifs • Small scissors • Metal ruler • Pencil • PVA (white) glue • Craft (utility) knife • Two-step crackle varnish • Hairdryer •
Kitchen paper • White spirit (paint thinner) • Oil-based varnish

7 Seal the the surface by brushing on 5–10 layers of water-based varnish. Allow each coat to dry throughly before applying the next.

9 Brush on the second stage of the crackle varnish, making sure that you have covered all areas. Leave to dry naturally for about 1–2 hours.

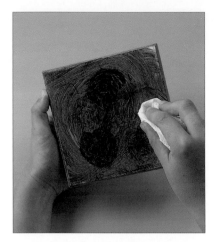

11 Put a tiny amount of raw umber oil paint on to a piece of kitchen paper moistened with white spirit and wipe over all surfaces of the box.

8 Following the manufacturer's instructions, brush on the first stage of the crackle varnish and leave until slightly tacky to the touch (about 1–2 hours, although this can vary).

10 If no cracks have appeared, use a hairdryer on its lowest setting and move it over the surface until the cracks begin to appear.

12 Take a clean sheet of kitchen paper and wipe off the excess, leaving the paint only in the cracks. Leave to dry overnight. Varnish with two coats of oil-based varnish. Screw the lid and base of the box back together.

CALLIGRAPHY CANDLESTICK

This elegant candlestick with its calligraphy decoupage and gilded details would look stylish in both a contemporary or more traditional setting. Fashionably distressed gilding adds extra effect. Both these techniques would work equally well on a wooden lamp base.

1 Paint the candlestick with a coat of acrylic primer and leave to dry. Sand lightly. Apply two layers of reddish-brown emulsion paint on the top and base sections of the candlestick only (this is the base for the gilding) and leave to dry.

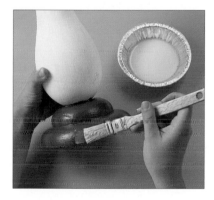

2 Apply a thin layer of water-based size over the painted top and base sections of the candlestick. Leave until the milky colour turns clear.

3 Cut some wedge-shaped pieces of Dutch metal leaf to fit the curve of the base. Press these on so that they overlap all the way around, removing the waxed backing as you go. Cover the top section in the same way, cutting pieces of leaf to fit the shape you are gilding.

4 Using a gilder's mop, gently smooth down the leaf with the side of the brush. Ensure that all the leaf has adhered, but do not remove the surplus leaf. Leave overnight to dry. Using the gilder's mop, remove the surplus leaf from the dried base and top with a circular motion.

5 To distress the leaf, remove a small amount using a wad of fine-grade wire wool. Drag over the leaf in one direction, being careful not to press too hard. Repeat with the top section.

Materials and Equipment You Will Need

Wooden candlestick • Small decorator's paintbrush • Acrylic primer • Fine-grade abrasive paper • Reddish-brown emulsion (latex) paint •
Water-based size • Small scissors • Dutch metal leaf • Gilder's mop (tip) • Fine-grade wire (steel) wool • Kitchen paper •
White spirit (paint thinner) • Shellac • Calligraphy paper • PVA (white) glue • Water-based acrylic varnish • Oil-based varnish

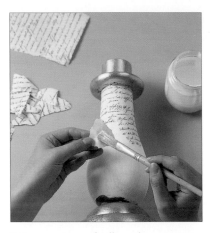

6 Using a piece of kitchen paper moistened with white spirit, gently wipe over the leaf to remove any dust particles. The white spirit will remove some of the leaf, allowing some of the reddish-brown primer to show through and creating an aged look.

8 Tear up pieces of calligraphy paper into different sizes and shapes to fit the curves of the candlestick. Stick on in a random fashion using diluted PVA glue until the main body of the candlestick is covered and there are no gaps. Leave to dry.

7 Seal the leaf with a coat of shellac. Leave to dry for about an hour.

9 Seal the decoupage with water-based varnish, applying enough layers to cover the ridges of the overlapping paper. Allow the candlestick to dry thoroughly. Finish with 1–2 coats of oil-based varnish over the calligraphy area only.

SEVENTIES LAMP BASE

Transform a plain lamp base into a stylish statement with this simple and evocative geometric design. It features wood veneer paper, one of the many modern materials you can use for an unusual decoupage effect.

2 Trace the templates from the back of the book or draw your own to size. Cut out the shapes from three shades of wood veneer. For each ellipse, also cut out a small oval shape to fit inside the aperture.

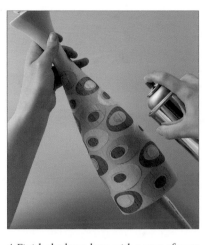

1 If the lamp base you are using has been varnished, gently sand it to reveal the natural wood underneath.

3 Plan the design by sticking the shapes to the lamp base with masking tape. When you are satisfied that the balance of colours is right, stick the shapes to the base with a glue stick, making sure the glue reaches to the edges. Quickly wipe away any excess with a piece of kitchen paper.

4 Finish the lamp base with a coat of matt polyurethane spray varnish. When dry, repeat with a second coat.

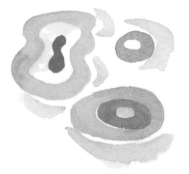

Materials and Equipment You Will Need
Wooden lamp base • Fine-grade abrasive paper • Pencil • Tracing paper • Fine pointed scissors • Wood veneer in three different natural wood shades • Masking tape • Glue stick • Kitchen paper • Matt (flat) polyurethane spray varnish

KITCHEN TABLE

This fun item of furniture will be the focal point of your kitchen. This wonderful table is decorated with cutlery and crockery images, using magazine cuttings and photographs enlarged on a photocopier. The bright paint colours add to the pleasing overall effect.

1 Apply a layer of undercoat to the entire table. When dry, apply 2–3 coats of yellow emulsion paint as a base, allowing each coat to dry before applying the next. Leave the table to dry.

2 Mark a border of squares about 5cm (2in) in from the outer edge of the table top. The size of the squares will depend on your images and the size of the table.

3 Draw a square the same size as the border squares on a sheet of paper. Following the pencil lines, cut out a stencil from acetate using a craft knife, metal ruler and cutting mat.

Materials and Equipment You Will Need
Large paintbrush • Undercoat • Wooden table • Yellow emulsion (latex) paint • Ruler • Pencil • Paper • Stencil acetate • Craft (utility) knife •
Metal ruler • Cutting mat • Acrylic paint, in pale blue and green • Stencil brush • Colour photographs of cutlery • Small scissors •
Dinner plate images from magazines • Craft (utility) knife • PVA (white) glue • Sponge or cloth • Clear acrylic spray varnish

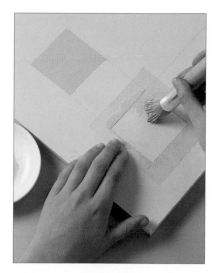

4 Take up a little blue paint on a stencil brush. Place the stencil over a square and apply the paint, using a dabbing motion. Stencil alternate blue squares.

6 Photograph colour images of cutlery. Then photocopy the images using a colour photocopier. Enlarge the images to the desired size.

8 Cut around the outline of the dinner plate images. If there are any areas that are too small to deal with, cut them away carefully with a craft knife.

5 When the blue squares are completely dry, stencil green ones in between in the same way.

7 Cut out the knife, fork and spoon images using small scissors. Carefully cut in between the tines of the fork motifs.

9 Apply PVA glue to the back of each cutlery image in turn. Place them end to end around the outer border. ▶

10 Glue the smaller dinner plate images on to the stencilled squares. Tamp down each one with a damp sponge or cloth to ensure that all the edges are stuck firmly and that there are no trapped air bubbles.

11 When the glue is completely dry, apply 2–3 coats of clear acrylic spray varnish to seal and protect the decoupage.

LIME GREEN PLANTER

Mix black and white border motifs with coloured flowers cut from wrapping paper to decorate an indoor plant pot. The vivid lime green background sets off the decoupage design beautifully. Use this striking container for all types of plants and foliage.

1 Paint the pot with lime green emulsion paint. Apply at least two coats for good coverage. Leave to dry between each coat.

2 Photocopy the required number of border motifs and carefully cut them out. Mix the wallpaper paste according to the manufacturer's instructions. Plan the border design using reusable adhesive.

3 When you are happy with the layout, paste the border motifs on to the pot. Leave to dry. Cut out floral motifs from wrapping paper and position each with reusable adhesive. Paste the flowers in place and leave to dry.

4 Apply several coats of oil-based varnish to protect the design and allow to dry.

5 Following the manufacturer's instructions, brush on a thin, even layer of the first stage of the crackle varnish and leave until tacky. Brush on one coat of the second stage of crackle varnish. Add a second coat. If no cracks appear, encourage them by moving a hairdryer on its lowest setting over the surface.

6 Put a tiny amount of raw umber oil paint on to a wad of kitchen paper moistened with white spirit and wipe it over the surface of the pot. Take a clean, soft cloth and wipe off the excess, leaving the paint only in the cracks. Leave to dry overnight. Finish with several coats of oil-based varnish.

Materials and Equipment You Will Need

Large terracotta pot • Medium decorator's paintbrush • Lime green emulsion (latex) paint • Photocopied border motifs • Scissors • Wallpaper paste • Reusable adhesive • Floral wrapping paper • Oil-based varnish • Two-step crackle varnish • Hairdryer • Raw umber artist's oil paint • Kitchen paper • White spirit (paint thinner) • Soft cloth

FLORAL PHOTOGRAPH FRAME

Help a tired picture frame burst back into life with these cheerful spring flowers. Seed and bulb catalogues are an excellent source of material for decoupage. This colourful design also features stylized leaf shapes cut out of plain green paper.

1 Paint the frame white to cover any existing finish. Cut a rectangle of tissue paper 2cm (1in) larger all around than the frame (including the depth) and glue it centrally to the front with diluted PVA glue. Glue the overlap around the edges, mitring the corners carefully.

2 Make a diagonal cut at each corner of the opening. Fold the surplus triangles to the back and glue in place, using an artist's paintbrush. Add a second layer if the paper is translucent.

3 Cut out a selection of flowers from the seed and bulb catalogues, in a variety of colours and shapes.

4 Trace the leaf templates from the back of the book on to the green paper and cut out several of each size in both colours.

5 Arrange the leaves and flowers around the frame, taking time to create a well-balanced design. Glue in place, then seal the surface with a coat of diluted PVA glue. Allow to dry, then finish with a coat of spray matt varnish.

Materials and Equipment You Will Need

Picture frame • Small decorator's paintbrush • White emulsion (latex) paint • Small scissors • Handmade tissue paper • PVA (white) glue • Medium artist's paintbrush • Seed and bulb catalogues • Tracing paper • Pencil • Two shades of green paper • Spray matt (flat) varnish

ZEBRA CHEST-OF-DRAWERS

Transform a dull piece of furniture with this striking black and white design and make a bold statement in any room. Bold zebra print paper is enlarged to different sizes on a photocopier, and used with smaller images of zebras copied from copyright-free books.

1 Prepare the surface of the chest-of-drawers, 'keying' the finish with abrasive paper. Remove the handles and set aside. Apply a coat of primer and leave to dry. Paint the edges of the chest with black emulsion paint. Leave to dry.

3 Mix the wallpaper paste following the manufacturer's instructions. Photocopy the required number of copyright-free border motifs and carefully cut each one out with scissors. Paste them around the edges of the drawers.

5 Arrange the motifs on each drawer front. When you are satisfied with the arrangement, stick each motif in place with wallpaper paste. Remove any air bubbles with a small roller, then allow to dry thoroughly.

2 Paint all the other facets of the chest, including the drawer fronts, white. Apply at least two coats and leave to dry thoroughly between each coat.

4 For the drawer fronts, photocopy the required number of zebra motifs from a copyright-free book, or cut them out from wrapping paper.

6 Enlarge panels of the zebra print paper on a photocopier or using a computer and scanner. Paste them in place to fit the sides of the chest.

Materials and Equipment You Will Need

Chest-of-drawers • Abrasive paper • Medium decorator's paintbrush • Primer • Emulsion (latex) paint, in black and white • Wallpaper paste • Border motifs • Small scissors • Glue stick • Zebra motifs • Small roller • Zebra print paper • Pencil • Water-based varnish • Two-step crackle varnish • Raw umber artist's oil paint • Soft cloth • White spirit (paint thinner) • Oil-based varnish

7 Use the roller to press out excess wallpaper paste from beneath the paper and to ensure there are no trapped air bubbles. Leave to dry.

9 Apply 6–10 layers of water-based varnish to the entire surface of the chest-of-drawers. Allow to dry thoroughly between each coat.

11 Put a tiny amount of raw umber oil paint on to a soft cloth, moistened with white spirit, and wipe the cloth over the entire chest.

8 Cut out more border motifs and stick them smoothly around the sides of the chest with wallpaper paste. Leave to dry.

10 Brush on a thin, even coat of the first stage of the crackle varnish. When it is tacky, brush on two layers of the second stage of the crackle varnish and leave to dry.

12 With a clean soft cloth, wipe off the excess white spirit, leaving the paint only in the cracks. Leave to dry overnight. ▶

13 Paint the drawer handles with two coats of black emulsion paint. Leave to dry between each coat.

15 Glue the paper circles to the surface of the handles with wallpaper paste. Dry.

17 Apply the first stage of crackle varnish and allow to dry. Apply two coats of the second stage. Allow to dry.

14 Reduce the zebra print on a photocopier or using a computer. Place the drawer handles on the paper and draw round them using a pencil. Cut out the circles.

16 Varnish the handles with 6–10 coats of oil-based varnish.

18 Antique the handles in the same way as the body of the chest by repeating steps 11 and 12. When dry, attach the handles to the chest. Finish with two coats of oil-based varnish over all surfaces.

STATIONERY BOX

Give a plain storage box or shoe box a personal touch by covering it with hand-written scraps from old letters. It is ideal for keepsakes or private correspondence. The different shades of notepaper create an attractive pastel design.

1 Cut the hand-written letters into squares of about 3cm (1½in).

2 Glue the squares to the box lid, alternating the direction of the writing to create a 'woven' effect.

4 Finish by spraying the box and lid with matt varnish. Once dry, apply a second coat for extra protection.

3 Cover the main box in the same way, then seal the surface of the box with diluted PVA glue.

Materials and Equipment You Will Need

Hand-written letters • Scissors • Cardboard box, with lid • PVA (white) glue • Large artist's paintbrush • Scissors • Spray matt (flat) varnish

ELEGANT BOX

Decoupaged with cornucopia and swags, this box has a classic, traditional look. Whether used to hold trinkets in the bedroom or letters on a bureau, its subtle colouring would blend well with many different settings.

1 Unscrew the box lid. Paint the top and base with acrylic primer. When dry, sand lightly and follow with two coats of pale yellow emulsion paint. Finish with a coat of acrylic varnish.

2 Mix a small amount of raw umber and gold acrylic paints with a little water, until it reaches the consistency of double (heavy) cream. Lay a coachliner brush in the paint, turning it over to ensure that it is well coated. Lay the brush on the edge of the box and draw it towards you, lifting it up gradually as you approach the end. Do the same for the edge of the box lid. Leave to dry.

3 To antique and seal the motifs and border, mix a little shellac with some sanding sealer. Add a little methylated spirits to make it easier to apply. Brush on, making each stroke in the same direction. Leave to dry.

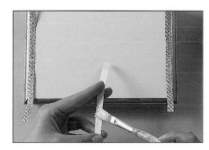

4 Cut out the designs. Take a strip of narrow border and centre it on the edge of the box lid. Glue just the centre down. Continue around the edges of the lid in the same way.

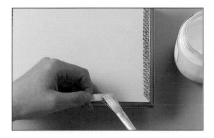

5 Place a metal ruler at an angle across the corner of the box lid. Take a craft knife and score the border at the corner sharply. Repeat with the remaining corners, then glue all the borders down firmly.

6 Take the main motif and place it in the middle of the lid. Use the ruler to measure the distance from the outer edge of the motif to the borders to make sure it is centred. Glue in position.

Materials and Equipment You Will Need

Small wooden box • Screwdriver • Small decorator's paintbrush • Acrylic primer • Abrasive paper • Pale yellow emulsion (latex) paint • Water-based varnish • Artist's acrylic paints, in raw umber and gold • Coachliner (liner) brush • Fruit and swag motifs and borders • Shellac • Sanding sealer • Methylated spirits (alcohol) • Scissors • PVA (white) glue • Large artist's paintbrush • Metal ruler • Craft (utility) knife • Water-based acrylic varnish • Two-step crackle varnish • Hairdryer • Raw umber artist's oil paint • Kitchen paper • White spirit (paint thinner) • Oil-based varnish

7 Glue a wide border around the bottom edge of the lid, using the pattern to cut and join pieces together. Glue the remaining motifs around the sides of the box base, using a ruler to make sure they are centred. Leave the box to dry.

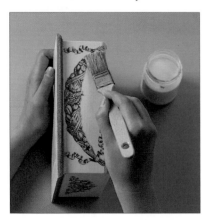

8 Apply 5–10 layers of water-based varnish and allow to dry thoroughly between each coat.

9 Brush on a thin, even layer of the first stage of the crackle varnish and leave until tacky, about 1–2 hours.

10 Brush on a layer of the second stage of crackle varnish and leave to dry completely. If no cracks appear, encourage them by moving a hairdryer on its lowest setting over the surface.

11 Put a tiny amount of raw umber oil paint on to a wad of kitchen paper moistened with white spirit and wipe over the entire box and lid. Take a clean piece of kitchen paper and wipe off the excess, leaving the paint only in the cracks. Leave to dry overnight.

12 Finish with two layers of oil-based varnish to protect the crackle varnish. Put the box back together.

TOY CHEST

This colourful child's toy chest started life as a rusting metal box, but, with a little time and effort, it has been transformed into something special. Similar neglected objects can be brought back to life in the same way, to make useful and beautiful heirlooms for the future.

1 Take time over the preparation of old metal, or you will have recurring problems with rust later on. Take a wire brush and rub any loose surface rust off the chest. Wash the chest with warm, soapy water, drying it well. Leave it to dry.

2 Apply a coat of red oxide metal primer and leave to dry.

3 Apply three coats of acrylic primer, or sufficient to cover the red oxide primer, and leave to dry. Alternatively, paint on one coat of acrylic primer followed by two coats of white vinyl silk emulsion paint. Allow to dry.

4 Make a glaze, using equal amounts of yellow emulsion paint and PVA glue and a little water until you achieve the translucency required. It is important to mix up enough of the mixture for the entire project as it is almost impossible to match the colour exactly should you have to mix up more. If you have any left over, it can be stored in a screwtop jar and used again.

5 Dampen a sponge and dip it into the glaze, then remove the surplus on kitchen paper. Dab the sponge all over the surface of the box, recharging it as necessary. Leave to dry, then protect with acrylic varnish.

6 Mix raw umber and gold paint with a little water. Using a coachliner, highlight the box rims. ▶

Materials and Equipment You Will Need
Stiff wire brush • Metal chest • Medium decorator's paintbrush • Red oxide metal primer • White acrylic primer •
Yellow emulsion (latex) paint (optional) • PVA (white) glue • Natural sponge • Kitchen paper • Water-based acrylic varnish •
Artist's acrylic paint, in raw umber and gold • Coachliner (liner) brush • Scissors • Colourful nursery motifs • Reusable adhesive •
Medium artist's paintbrush • Oil-based satin varnish

7 Cut out the motifs and, using reusable adhesive, arrange them all over the box, making sure that they are evenly spaced. Position small motifs around the edges of the box.

9 When the glue is dry, apply at least eight coats of water-based varnish to the box to withstand the rigours of the playroom, allowing each coat to dry before applying the next.

8 Glue the motifs in place, using PVA glue and an artist's paintbrush.

10 Finish with two coats of oil-based satin varnish.

SOUVENIR TRAY

Make sure your vacation memories stay fresh in your mind with this imaginative tray. It's a clever way to transform a dilapidated tray and would make an ideal gift. Choose a strong background colour to hold the design together.

1 If the tray is already painted, varnished or waxed, 'key' the finish using fine-grade abrasive paper. Spray the tray with two evenly applied layers of dark blue paint, making sure that it is covered completely.

2 Photocopy your collection of travel ephemera, reducing the scale slightly if desired. Cut out each item.

3 Arrange the cut-outs on the tray. When you are satisfied, stick them down with PVA glue.

4 Seal the surface with a coat of diluted PVA glue. When the first coat of varnish is completely dry, apply a second coat for extra protection.

Materials and Equipment You Will Need
Wooden tray • Fine-grade abrasive paper • Dark blue spray paint • Collection of labels, tickets, postcards, etc • Scissors • PVA (white) glue • Matt (flat) spray varnish

GILDED MIRROR

This sumptuous frame is achieved by applying ornate black and white borders on top of Dutch metal leaf. Artful distressing gives the gold an antique look and lends a classical touch to a favourite piece. This technique could be equally effective on a picture frame.

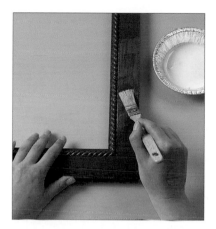

4 Using a gilder's mop or very soft brush, gently remove the surplus leaf with a circular motion.

1 Take the mirror glass out of the frame. If this is not possible, place masking tape along the mirror glass, right up against the wood of the frame. Prepare the surface of the frame, then apply a layer of acrylic primer. Leave to dry, then sand. Follow with two coats of reddish-brown emulsion paint, sanding between coats to achieve a really smooth finish. This is particularly important, as any flaws will show up on the gilding. Brush on a thin, even layer of water-based size and leave until it begins to go clear and is slightly tacky.

2 Beginning with the flat areas of the frame, cut pieces of metal leaf to fit, making them slightly larger than required. Lay them on the frame, overlapping each one. Smooth them down with your fingers, then remove the waxed backing. Repeat until all the flat areas are covered.

3 Cut strips of leaf to fit the raised areas. Take the pieces of leaf and press them down on the raised areas, using the waxed backing to smooth them into the crevices. Remove the backing. If the leaf has not gone into the crevices but you want to cover these areas, dab on a little bronze powder using the end of a very fine brush. Leave the frame to dry overnight.

5 Gently rub the raised areas and edges of the frame with fine-grade wire wool to antique it. Moisten a piece of kitchen paper with white spirit and clean off the dust left by the wire wool. ▶

Materials and Equipment You Will Need
Mirror • Masking tape (optional) • Medium decorator's paintbrush • Acrylic primer • Abrasive paper • Reddish-brown emulsion (latex) paint • Water-based size • Scissors • Dutch metal leaf • Bronze powder (optional) • Gilder's mop (tip) or very soft brush • Fine-grade wire (steel) wool • Kitchen paper • White spirit (paint thinner) • Shellac or sanding sealer • Border motif • Methylated spirits (alcohol) • Metal ruler • Pencil • PVA (white) glue • Medium artist's paintbrush • Craft (utility) knife • Water-based varnish

6 Seal the leaf with a coat of shellac or sanding sealer.

8 Cut out the borders, starting with the centre of the design, then cut round the outer edges.

10 Mitre the corners (see Basic Techniques). Remove the loose pieces and stick down the remaining edges. Leave to dry thoroughly.

7 Estimate how the border motif will fit round the frame, and how many joins you need to make. Photocopy the required number of borders, adjusting the size if necessary. Seal and antique the borders using a little sanding sealer tinted with a little shellac, and mixed with a little methylated spirits.

9 Using a metal ruler, find the centre point of the frame and mark lightly with a pencil. Take the first border, centre it and glue to hold the middle in place while you position the rest.

11 To finish the frame and protect the gilding, apply 5–10 layers of water-based varnish. Leave to dry completely.

BUTLER'S TRAY

This tray will provide a talking point as well as lending a classical air to any room. Combining good looks with practicality, it is perfect for a game of chess after serving the drinks! This design would look equally effective on a small occasional table.

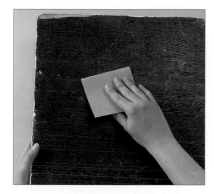

1 Remove any previous paint from the tray with abrasive paper, then sand the surface of the tray smooth to provide a 'key' for the new paint.

2 Apply two coats of undercoat and one of yellow top coat, leaving to dry between each layer.

3 Photocopy the required number of border patterns and cut them out. Mix the wallpaper paste according to the manufacturer's instructions, and paste the borders around the inside and outside edges of the tray, matching the pattern as necessary.

4 Soak the design in water to stretch the paper. When the design dries it will shrink, drying taut on the inside of the tray.

5 Paste the chessboard design in the centre of the tray, with a white square in the bottom right-hand corner. Use a small roller to remove any excess paste. ▶

Materials and Equipment You Will Need

Butler's tray • Abrasive paper • Medium decorator's paintbrush • Yellow undercoat • Yellow emulsion (latex) paint • Border patterns • Scissors • Wallpaper paste • Chessboard design • Small roller • Corner motifs and floral motifs • Water-based varnish • Two-step crackle varnish • Hairdryer • Raw umber artist's oil paint • White spirit (paint thinner) • Soft cloth • Oil-based varnish

6 Paste a border around the edge of the chessboard design. Add extra motifs at the corners and floral motifs to fill any gaps.

7 Brush on at least six coats of varnish and allow to dry. Brush on a thin, even layer of the first stage of the crackle varnish and leave until tacky. Then brush on a layer of the second stage and leave to dry. If no cracks appear, encourage them by moving a hairdryer on its lowest setting over the surface (see Basic Techniques).

8 Put a little raw umber oil paint on to a soft cloth moistened with white spirit and wipe over the entire surface. Take a clean, soft cloth and wipe off the excess, leaving the paint only in the cracks. Leave to dry overnight. Finish with two coats of oil-based varnish.

LIBRARY WASTEBASKET

This wastebasket is far too attractive to hide under a desk! Images of books are the perfect design for a study or home office. The shapes are cut out of wrapping paper and then re-assembled to look like a library around the shape of the wastebasket.

1 Paint the inside of the wastebasket black, applying two coats of matt emulsion (latex) paint. Leave to dry.

2 Cut out images of books from wrapping paper, either individually or in groups.

3 Soak the images in water for no more than a minute to stretch the paper.

4 Mix the wallpaper paste according to the manufacturer's instructions and thinly cover one side of the wastebasket.

5 Paste the large book images to the top half. Align the raw edge with the edge of the wastebasket. Overlap the paper so that it wraps around the sides.

6 Use a small roller to press out excess paste from underneath the paper. ▶

Materials and Equipment You Will Need

Plain wastebasket • Medium decorator's paintbrush • Black matt emulsion (flat latex) paint • Scissors • Wrapping paper featuring images of books • Wallpaper paste • Small roller • Edging motifs • Water-based varnish • Two-step crackle varnish • Hairdryer • Raw umber artist's oil paint • Soft white cloth • White spirit (paint thinner) • Oil-based varnish

7 Arrange the smaller book images at the base of the wastebasket. Place books horizontally and vertically to cover the surface. Soak and glue in place as before.

9 Repeat, adding decorative corners and borders to the sides and bottom of the wastebasket to achieve the desired effect.

11 Brush on a thin, even coat of the crackle varnish and leave until tacky. Brush on two coats of the second stage of crackle varnish, the second coat about 30 minutes after the first, and leave to dry completely. If no cracks appear, encourage them by moving a hairdryer on its lowest setting over the surface (see Basic Techniques).

8 Photocopy an edging motif and cut out. Paste it to the top of the wastebasket, overlapping the book paper. Fold over the top edge of the basket. Trim the edging at the sides flush with the edges of the bin. Apply a layer of water-based varnish.

10 Apply 6–10 coats of water-based varnish to the entire surface, inside and out, allowing to dry between each coat.

12 Put a tiny amount of raw umber oil paint on to a soft cloth moistened with white and wipe over the bin. Wipe off the excess, leaving the paint only in the cracks. Leave to dry overnight. Varnish the wastebasket inside and out with 6–10 coats of oil-based varnish.

PAPER PATCHWORK ALBUM

This simple idea is a fun, inexpensive way to make a striking album cover. The unusual decoupage is inspired by one of the star motifs found on antique patchwork quilts. The simple blue and white colour theme is made interesting by the use of different patterns.

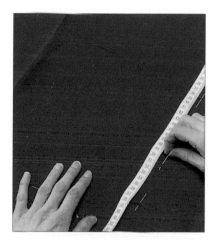

1 Trace the diamond and triangle templates at the back of the book to the size required. Cut out eight diamonds and eight triangles from the blue and white wrapping paper and envelopes, and eight triangles from plain white paper.

2 Lightly draw two pencil lines on a piece of coloured paper to divide it in half vertically and horizontally. Using a glue stick, glue the diamonds and triangles into a design, using the pencil lines as a guide. Erase any visible pencil marks.

3 Using all six strands of embroidery thread, sew a button through the paper to the outer point of each diamond and one to the centre of the star. Secure the ends of the thread to the wrong side with masking tape. ▶

Materials and Equipment You Will Need

Tracing paper • Pencil • Scissors • Blue and white patterned wrapping paper • Envelopes with blue and white patterned reverse side • Sheet of white paper • Two sheets of coloured paper • Ruler • Glue stick • Eraser • Embroidery needle • Blue stranded embroidery thread (floss) • 9 Pearl buttons • Masking tape • Two rectangles of thick cardboard • Metal ruler • Craft (utility) knife • Three bulldog clips • Leather hole punch • Narrow blue and white striped ribbon

4 Score a line 3cm (1½in) from one short end of each piece of card, using a metal ruler and craft knife.

5 Glue a sheet of coloured paper to one piece of card to make the back cover. For the front cover, glue the patchwork design to the other piece of card.

6 Clip together the sheets of drawing paper. Mark two points, each 2cm (¾in) from the short side and 6cm (2½in) down from each long edge, and punch through these marks. Make holes in the front and back covers in the same positions.

7 Sandwich the paper between the two covers and thread together with ribbon. Knot tightly and tie the ends in a bow.

PAISLEY EGGS

These beautifully patterned eggs are eye-catching ornaments and would make a striking centrepiece for an Easter table.
Decorate just one, or make a feature out of a basket of eggs covered in complementary colours and patterns.

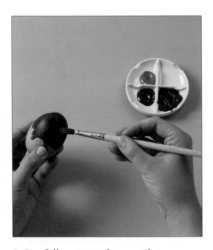

2 Cut out paisley motifs in different sizes from the wrapping paper.

1 Carefully paint each egg with two even layers of craft paint, choosing a colour that complements the patterned wrapping paper.

4 Coat the egg with several layers of nail polish, allowing each to dry completely before applying the next. Cover one end of the egg at a time and place it in an egg cup while the polish dries.

3 Glue the motifs on to the egg in a pattern, using PVA glue. Seal with a coat of diluted PVA.

Materials and Equipment You Will Need
Wooden eggs • Medium artist's paintbrush • Craft paints • Small scissors • Paisley-patterned wrapping paper • PVA (white) glue •
Clear nail polish • Egg cup

BOTANICAL CHEST

Give a plain pine chest a new lease of life with this fresh, botanical design. Silver paint makes an unusual and very attractive base for decoupage. Here the botanical images are coloured with pearlized paints to add to the delicate overall effect.

1 Photocopy botanical images in different sizes in black and white. Paint them with diluted pearlized paint.

2 When the paint is dry, cut out the individual plants.

3 Sand any rough edges on the chest to create a smooth surface. Fill any holes with wood filler. ▶

Materials and Equipment You Will Need

Botanical images • Fine artist's paintbrush • Pearlized paint • Small scissors • Abrasive paper • Plain wooden chest • Wood filler (optional) • Medium decorator's paintbrush • Neutral-coloured emulsion (latex) paint • Silver spray paint • Newspaper • Masking tape • Wallpaper paste • Small roller • Baking parchment • Matt (flat) polyurethane varnish

4 Paint the chest with emulsion primer. Use a neutral colour to complement the silver paint.

5 Photocopy an edging motif and cut out. Paste it to the top of the wastebasket, overlapping the book paper. Fold over the top edge of the basket. Trim the edging at the sides flush with the edges of the bin. Apply a layer of water-based varnish.

6 Mix the wallpaper paste according to the manufacturer's instructions. Plan the design with masking tape, then stick down the cut-outs. Use a small roller to press out excess paste from beneath the motifs. Leave to dry thoroughly.

7 Rub the chest with baking parchment, then varnish the decoupage with several coats of matt polyurethane varnish, allowing each coat to dry completely before applying the next. Reassemble the chest once the final coat is dry.

Above: Black and white photocopies of copyright-free images are good source material for decoupage.

ANTIQUED FIRESCREEN

A firescreen provides a useful and decorative cover-up for an empty fireplace in the warmer months. In this design, irregular shapes are fitted together like crazy paving, leaving an outline of space around each image.

1 Position the firescreen so that the feet hang over the edge of your painting table. Apply a coat of acrylic primer on the feet only, followed by two coats of cream emulsion paint. Finish with a coat of water-based varnish. Stand the screen upright and, painting first one side and then the other, apply a coat of primer. Sand lightly when it is dry, then apply two coats of cream emulsion and a coat of water-based varnish.

2 Mix some raw umber and gold acrylic paint with a little water to make a sloppy consistency. Place the screen flat and, using a coachliner brush, paint a narrow border all the way round the edge, using the edge of the screen as a guide. Using an artist's paintbrush, apply the same paint on the front edges of the feet. When dry, turn over and paint the back edges of the feet.

3 Cut out suitable motifs from the wallpaper or wrapping paper.

4 Using small pieces of reusable adhesive, arrange the motifs on the screen to fit loosely together, leaving a small gap all round each piece. You will find that you need to experiment with moving the images around until you are satisfied with the way they fit together.

5 When you are completely happy with the arrangement, stick all the pieces in place with diluted PVA glue.

6 Lay the screen down flat to varnish it, as this will help to minimize any drips. Apply 5–10 layers of water-based acrylic varnish and allow to dry. ▶

Materials and Equipment You Will Need
Firescreen • Medium decorator's paintbrush • Acrylic primer • Cream emulsion (latex) paint • Water-based acrylic varnish • Abrasive paper • Artist's acrylic paints, in raw umber and gold • Coachliner (liner) brush • Medium artist's paintbrush • Small scissors • Wallpaper or wrapping paper • Reusable adhesive • PVA (white) glue • Two-step crackle varnish • Hairdryer • Kitchen paper • White spirit (paint thinner) • Satin-finish oil-based varnish

7 Brush on a thin, even layer of the first stage of the crackle varnish, ensuring that the screen is covered. Leave to dry until slightly tacky, about 1–3 hours.

9 Put a tiny amount of raw umber oil paint on to a piece of kitchen paper moistened with white spirit and wipe over the surface of the firescreen. Take a clean piece of kitchen paper and wipe off the excess, leaving the paint only in the cracks. Leave to dry overnight.

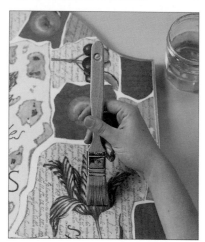

8 Brush on an even layer of the second stage of the crackle varnish. If, after about an hour no cracks have appeared, move a hairdryer on its coolest setting over the surface of the whole screen (see Basic Techniques).

10 Apply two thin layers of satin-finish, oil-based varnish over both sides of the firescreen, and the feet.

STRAWBERRY TEA TRAY

This tea tray has a lovely summery feel to it, and is perfect for taking tea outdoors on a sunny day. Enlarge or reduce a single strawberry motif on a black and white photocopier to give a range of sizes then apply randomly over the surface.

1 If the tray is already painted or varnished but in reasonable condition, 'key' the surface with abrasive paper. If the tray has been waxed, it must be removed using fine grade wire wool moistened with white spirit. Paint on two layers of acrylic primer, sanding each coat lightly once it is dry.

2 Mix up a small amount of glaze using equal quantities of pale blue emulsion paint and PVA glue, adding about twice the amount of water. Paint the glaze on evenly, then wipe off the excess paint from your brush and drag it along the surface to reveal parallel lines. Continue in this way, stopping to wipe the excess paint off the brush, until the tray is covered. Leave to dry and seal with a layer of varnish.

3 Using a coachliner brush, paint around the rim of the tray.

4 While the paint is drying, tint the motifs using coloured pencils. Seal with sanding sealer. Leave to dry for about 30 minutes.

5 Cut out the motifs and arrange them over the surface of the tray, interspersing large strawberries with smaller ones. Use small motifs to decorate the outer and inner edges and large ones around the outer edges. Glue the motifs in place with PVA glue diluted with water.

6 Brush on between five and ten layers of acrylic varnish.

Materials and Equipment You Will Need

Small wooden tea tray • Abrasive paper • Medium decorator's paintbrush • Acrylic primer • Pale blue emulsion (latex) paint • PVA (white) glue • Water-based acrylic varnish • Coachliner (liner) brush • Large and small strawberry motifs • Coloured pencils • Sanding sealer • Small scissors • Medium artist's paintbrush

CHERUBIM HEADBOARD

Give a child's bedroom a heavenly feel with this fun cherubim headboard. White clouds and a blue sky make a dreamy setting for this design. Stencilling and sponging create a richly textured background for the decoupage of cherubim.

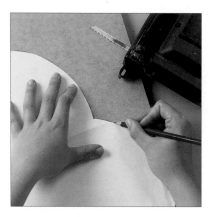

1 Wearing a protective face mask, cut out the sheet of MDF to fit the width of the bed. Roughly sketch a shaped outline for the top of the headboard on a large sheet of paper and cut out. Trace the template on to the sheet of MDF. Cut out the shape using a jigsaw, then sand the edge smooth.

2 Apply two or three coats of pale blue emulsion paint, allowing each coat to dry before applying the next.

3 Using a sponge, apply a little dark blue acrylic paint around the edges of the headboard, and more sparsely towards the centre, to create a mottled effect. Apply the lighter shade of blue acrylic paint in the same way.

Materials and Equipment You Will Need

Protective face mask • Saw • Sheet of 9mm (½in) thick MDF (medium-density fiberboard) • Pencil • Large sheet of paper • Large scissors • Tracing paper • Jigsaw (saber saw) • Abrasive paper • Large decorator's paintbrush • Pale blue emulsion (latex) paint • Small natural sponge • Acrylic paints, in dark- and mid-blue and white • Stencil acetate • Craft (utility) knife • Stencil brush • Cherub motifs in different sizes • PVA (white) glue and spreader • Soft white cloth • Fine artist's paintbrush • Clear acrylic spray varnish • 120cm (48in) length of 6cm (2½in) wide wooden batten (lath) • Drill • Screwdriver • Screws

4 Trace the cloud template at the back of the book on to paper. Following the pencil lines cut a stencil from acetate.

6 Cut out the cherub motifs. Use large scissors to remove excess paper and to cut out larger motifs.

8 Place the motifs face down on to a sheet of spare paper and apply PVA glue to the back of each one.

5 Pour out some white acrylic paint. Take up a little on a stencil brush and wipe off the excess. Place the cloud stencil along the shaped edge of the headboard and apply the paint with a dabbing motion to create fluffy clouds.

7 Use a craft knife to cut close to the edge of each image and for smaller, more intricate details.

9 Glue the large cherub images to the centre of the headboard, carefully smoothing each cut-out into position with a damp cloth to ensure that all edges are firmly stuck and there are no trapped air bubbles. ▶

10 Using a fine paintbrush, glue smaller cherubs on each side of the headboard to flank the central group.

12 Apply 2–3 coats of clear acrylic spray varnish to seal and protect the design.

11 Stencil more white clouds in a random fashion over the rest of the headboard.

13 Cut the wooden batten in half. Place these on the back of the headboard to form 'legs'. Drill pilot holes through the battens into the MDF then screw them into position.

VICTORIAN SCRAPS TABLE

This pretty occasional table would be handy in any room, whether used to hold a vase of flowers in the living room or books and a cup of tea in the bedroom. It is inspired by the Victorians' love of colourful scraps, which are still available today.

1 Apply a coat of primer to the table. Paint with black undercoat, then black emulsion paint. Allow to dry. Cut out a selection of scraps and arrange them on the table top.

2 Mix the wallpaper paste and apply to the table top. Stick the images in place, building up the design by overlapping them. Apply more paste over the top of the scraps. Use a roller to press out any excess paste. Allow to dry.

3 Cut out sufficient borders to line the side edges of the table. Paste in place.

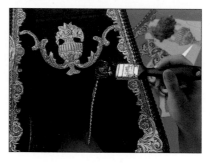

4 Decorate the sides of the table with borders and decorative motifs. Allow to dry, then apply several coats of water-based varnish.

5 Brush on a thin, even layer of the first stage of the crackle varnish and leave for 1–3 hours. Brush on two layers of the second stage, the second coat 30 minutes after the first coat, and leave to dry completely. If no cracks appear, encourage them by moving a hairdryer on its lowest setting over the surface.

6 Put a tiny amount of raw umber oil paint on to a wad of kitchen paper moistened with white spirit and wipe over the surface. Wipe off the excess with more paper, leaving the paint only in the cracks. Leave to dry.

7 Rub gold paint over any raised details with your finger to highlight the edge of the table. Allow to dry, then apply 6–10 coats of oil-based varnish.

Materials and Equipment You Will Need

Medium decorator's paintbrush • Black primer • Small wooden table • Black undercoat • Black emulsion (latex) paint • Small scissors • Victorian scraps • Wallpaper paste • Small roller • Border motifs • Water-based varnish • Two-step crackle varnish • Hairdryer • Raw umber artist's oil paint • Kitchen paper • White spirit (paint thinner) • Gold paint • Oil-based varnish

NAUTILUS BATHROOM CABINET

Paint a plain wooden cabinet and then add a decoupage design of large-scale sea shells to add a fresh look to any bathroom. The entire surface has been lightly aged. This simple design shows how effective large repeated motifs can be.

1 Paint the cupboard with a layer of acrylic primer. Leave to dry, then paint on two coats of cream emulsion paint. When dry, apply a coat of water-based acrylic varnish. Cut out the shell motifs from the wrapping paper.

2 Take a shell motif and position it so that part of it is in the recess of the door and part is on the outer rim. Run your fingernail along the edge to make sure that the paper is right up against the edge. Put a piece of reusable adhesive on the back. Position more motifs.

3 Stick all the shell motifs in place with PVA glue, diluted with water. Leave to dry completely. ▶

Materials and Equipment You Will Need

Wooden cupboard (cabinet) • Medium decorator's paintbrush • Acrylic primer • Cream emulsion (latex) paint • Water-based acrylic varnish • Scissors • Wrapping paper with shell motifs • Reusable adhesive • PVA (white) glue • Medium artist's paintbrush • Craft (utility) knife • Metal ruler • Raw umber artist's oil paint • White spirit (paint thinner) • Kitchen paper

4 If you have stuck motifs over the doors, use a craft knife and metal ruler to slit the image along the door edge and ensure that the door opens fully.

6 To antique the cupboard, take a little raw umber artist's oil paint and mix it with white spirit to the consistency of thin cream. Brush it on to the cupboard and leave for a few minutes.

7 Wipe off the liquid with kitchen paper before it dries, leaving a residue in the corners and as much or little as you like elsewhere. Leave to dry.

5 Brush on three layers of water-based varnish, leaving each coat to dry before applying the next.

8 Finish and protect the decorated cupboard with 5–10 more coats of water-based varnish.

IVY LEAF MIRROR

With its trailing ivy motifs, this elegant mirror frame would be perfect for a hallway, bedroom or conservatory.
Classical black and white borders and creamy-white flowers complete this lovely design scheme.

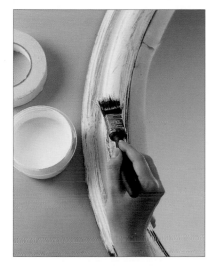

1 Place masking tape around the edge of the mirror glass to protect it. Apply two coats of undercoat followed by a top coat of white emulsion paint. Allow to dry between each coat.

2 Photocopy sufficient copyright-free borders, and cut out enough to go round the outer and inner edges of the mirror frame. Mix the wallpaper paste according to the manufacturer's instructions. Apply paste to the frame and stick on the borders, aligning and joining up the design as necessary.

3 Remove the layer of tissue from the back of each napkin. Cut around the ivy shapes, leaving a small border all around. Apply more paste to the mirror frame and stick the ivy shapes in place. ▶

Materials and Equipment You Will Need
Masking tape • Round or oval mirror • Small decorator's brush • White undercoat • White emulsion (latex) paint • Small scissors •
Black and white borders • Wallpaper paste • White paper napkins with ivy leaf design • Cream or white floral motifs • Water-based varnish •
Two-step crackle varnish • Hairdryer • Oil-based raw umber paint • Soft white cloths • White spirit (paint thinner) • Oil-based varnish

4 Cut out the floral images and paste on to the frame. Allow to dry.

5 Apply several coats of water-based varnish to protect the design. Leave to dry between each coat.

6 Following the manufacturer's instructions, brush on a thin, even layer of the first stage of the crackle varnish. Leave for 1–3 hours until tacky. Then brush on two layers of the second stage of the varnish, the second coat 30 minutes after the first, and leave to dry completely. If no cracks appear, encourage them by moving a hairdryer on its lowest setting over the surface.

7 Apply a small quantity of raw umber paint to a soft cloth. Add a little white spirit. Apply to the frame using a circular motion, then, with a clean cloth rub over the surface to remove the excess paint. The colour will remain in the cracks. Apply 6–10 coats of oil-based varnish to protect the surface.

TEMPLATES

If the templates need to be enlarged, either use a grid system or a photocopier. For the grid system, trace the template and draw a grid of evenly spaced squares over your tracing. To scale up, draw a large grid on to another piece of paper. Copy the outline on to the second square, taking each square individually and drawing the relevant part of the outline in the larger square. Finally, draw over the lines to make sure they are continuous. Alternatively, two different sizes of graph paper may be used.

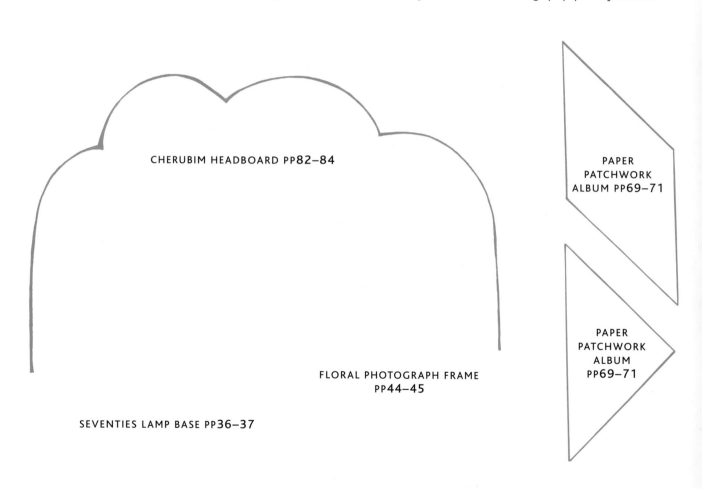

CHERUBIM HEADBOARD PP82–84

PAPER PATCHWORK ALBUM PP69–71

FLORAL PHOTOGRAPH FRAME PP44–45

PAPER PATCHWORK ALBUM PP69–71

SEVENTIES LAMP BASE PP36–37

SUPPLIERS

UK

A S Handover Ltd
374 Mildmay Grove
London N1 4RH
Tel: 0171 359 4696
for brushes and artists' materials

C Brewer & Sons Ltd
27 Bourne Way
Salisbury Business Centre
Salisbury SP1 2NY
Tel: 01722 412653
www.brewers.co.uk
for decorative materials

Caspari Ltd
9 Shire Hill Industrial Estate
Saffron Walden
Essex CB11 3AP
Tel: 01799 513010
for wrapping paper

David Beck Design
Frog Lane, Chilmark
Salisbury SP3 5BB
Tel: 01722 716804
for MDF blanks and furniture

Dover Street Bookshop
18 Earlham Street
London WC2H 9LN
Tel: 020 7836 2111
for copyright-free images

Falkiner Fine Papers
76 Southampton Row
London WC1B 4AR
Tel: 0171 831 1151
www.falkiners.com

Maggie Pryce
Decoupage and Gilded Gifts
39 Kingston Deverill

Warminster
Wiltshire BA12 7HE
Tel: 01985 844 402
www.maggiepryce.co.uk
*for handcrafted decoupage items
and varnishes*

Panduro Hobby Ltd
Freepost
Customer Service
SE-205 15 Malmö
Sweden
www.pandurohobby.co.uk
for frames, paints and varnishes

Paperchase
www.paperchase.co.uk
for handmade and decorative papers

Porter Design Ltd
The Old Estate Yard
Bath BA2 9BR
www.porter-design.com
for prints and wrapping paper

USA

Art Supply Warehouse
5325 Departure Drive
North Raleight, NC 27616
Tel: (919) 878-5077
www.aswexpress.com

Craft Catalog
P. O. Box 1069
Reynoldsburg, OH 43068
Tel: (800) 777 1442
www.craftcatalog.com

Craft King
P. O. Box 90637
Lakeland, FL 33804
Tel: (800) 769 9494
www.craft-king.com

Dick Blick Art Materials
P. O. Box 1267
695 US Highway 150 East
Galesburg, IL 61402
www.dickblick.com

Jerry's Artarama
1-800-U-ARTIST (827-8478)
PO Box 58638J, Raleigh, NC
27658-8638
www.jerrysartarama.com

Twinrocker Handmade Paper
POB 413
BROOKSTON, IN
47923
Tel: (800) 757 8946
www.twinrocker.com

Australia

A to Z Art Supplies
50 Brunswick Terrace
Wynn Vale, SA 5127
Tel: (08) 8289 1202

Art & Craft Warehouse
19 Main Street
Pialba, QLD 4655
Tel: (07) 4124 2581

Artland
272 Moggill Road
Indooroopilly, QLD 4068
Tel: (07) 3878 5536
Free call: 1800 81 5377
www.artlandindooroopilly.com.au

Bondi Road Art Supplies
181 Bondi Road
Bondi, NSW 2026
Tel: (02) 9386 1779
www.bondiroadartsupplies.
  com.au

Eckersleys
126 Commercial Road
Prahran, VIC 3181
Tel: (03) 9510 1418
www.eckersleys.com.au

Janet's Art Supplies & Books
145 Victoria Avenue
Chatswood, NSW 2067
Tel: (02) 9417 8572

Jacksons Drawing Supplies
Hay Street
Perth, WA 6000
Tel: (08) 9321 8707
www.jacksons.com.au

Oxford Art Supplies Pty Ltd
223 Oxford Street
Darlinghurst, NSW 2010
Tel: (02) 9360 4066
http://oxfordart.com.au

INDEX